The World Imagined

A shimmering rendering of an adopted child's odyssey on her long journey towards Home. Adopted at birth, Judith Slater grew up not only in a small town and its surrounding fields and woods, but also in the stories she spun to give her world emotional substance. She was born a fawn in a woodland clearing. She ministered to a tribe of miniature people who needed her help. She also learned from a farmer's gaggle of raucous children to run and wrestle and climb, tomboying herself from sickness to health. She grew into the dangerous teens. These strands and the thirst for a fuller sense of herself gave life to the real mission: the search for her birth mother.

Judith Slater has retrieved for us an enthralling tale of search and adventure, of loss and finding.

—Ann Goldsmith
No One is the Same Again, QRL Poetry Prize

Reading Judith Slater's tough-minded and moving memoir, I imagine a speaker haunted by two commandments: *Understand what you cannot accept* and *Accept what you cannot understand*. She seems to know quite clearly how these are not at all the same command, and the way that her narrative works through them gives me immense pleasure and hope.

—Max Wickert

The World Imagined

by

Judith F. Slater

Illustrations by Ruth Armstrong

Buffalo Arts Publishing

The World Imagined. Copyright © 2018 by Judith F. Slater. All rights reserved. Printed in the United States of America. No part of this book may be used or reproduced in any manner whatsoever without written permission from the publisher. For information, address Buffalo Arts Publishing, 179 Greenfield Drive, Tonawanda, NY 14150.

Email: info@buffaloartspublishing.com

ISBN 978-0997874150 | LCCN 2017964135

Cover painting: "Iroquois Heron" by Edward Bielicki.
All photographs from the author's collection.
Illustrations by Ruth Armstrong

Printed in the USA

For

My Grandchildren

Emma
Jake
Max
Delaney
Morgan

The World Imagined

Light the first light of evening, as in a room
In which we rest and, for small reason, think
The world imagined is the ultimate good.

This is, therefore, the intensest rendezvous.
It is in that thought that we collect ourselves,
Out of all the indifferences, into one thing.

—Wallace Stevens

Preface

This book is for anyone who has been a child born in a particular place at a certain time to people who may raise her or whom she may never get to know. It is about a child's world of fears, of enchantment and fantasy, adventures. All children seek to discover their place in the world. It can be more complex for the adopted child who, in a sense, is free to find that anywhere by pretending it exists, while fearing that it doesn't, or fearing it could as easily bring disgrace as fulfillment.

> *It is a child that sings itself to sleep,*
> *The mind, among the creatures that it makes,*
> *The people, those by which it lives and dies.*
>
> —Wallace Stevens

My Beginnings

I was not, as I was told, born
red and scabby, held under a faucet,
and slathered with oil
before being handed over.

I was born in a trampled bed
of ferns and shot into the world
glistening. A tongue cleaned me.
A moist nose nudged me upright.

That night, I watched lights
blinking around us and thought
I will like this place. I stumbled
before I learned to walk properly,

took the stairs at a bound,
my new mother cautioning,
"One at a time, Miss."
In games, my legs tangled

hopelessly, but in the woods
alone, I leapt ravines, rooted
and rolled freely. Whenever
I came upon a doe or fawns,

we exchanged long looks.
Once, against the fiery screen
of sunset, I glimpsed the outline
of a massive stag.

1938

A nineteen-year-old waits alone in a boarding house with her two-day-old infant whose body rash has been treated with cooking oil. A couple drives through an ice storm, the woman holding a hand-knit blue coat. In the years to come, this coat mended and stored in moth balls will clothe at least four generations of babies and baby dolls.

What are those three thinking as they make the exchange? As a child I ask my parents many times what my "other" mother looks like, but they can't tell me. They say that she did not make an impression; they were only looking at me.

Early Days

The toes of my first baby shoes are crumpled. There's a snapshot of me in those shoes, foot in mid-air, running from one pair of outstretched hands to another, a spaniel leaping beside me.

My mother's family is first-generation Scots and Swedish. Her father, a successful builder, has sent his daughters to a finishing school in D.C. and his son to engineering college. He employs a live-in immigrant maid, Molly, governed severely by my

Bud Fairbank and Grace Rogerson, Summer 1932

grandmother. Prominent in their community, the Rogersons occupy a front pew of the First Presbyterian, a church my grandfather built. They are also afflicted by depression and serious illnesses.

My father's family are farmers and shopkeepers, sturdy, down to earth, and humorous. We attend mostly Rogerson family gatherings:

> Late afternoon sun through beveled windows. Grandfather Rogerson presiding at the head of the large mahogany table—next to Grandmother, bosom sparkling with jewels, face flushed from hollering at Molly the red-faced, untidy cook: "put on a clean apron for godssake." On their right, their beloved and only son, Paul, face pained, eyes half-closed, slouching beside Myrtle, his glamorous wife. Then, me in an organdy dress, my brother scowling, mother glaring at our father, a few shots of Four Roses offsetting Rogerson gloom, anchoring the table's other end. Mother's sister Ethel twists her fingers and beams at her husband, the lieutenant colonel, on furlough and in full military dress. Beside him, two girl cousins giggle.

> Hair singed by the oven, Mollie bears in the turkey. Grandfather brandishing the antique knife, makes a shaky first cut. Molly lifts the platter and staggers around to my father, the butcher's boy, who casually disjoints the thighs and wings, slices the breast into perfect portions, &

pops a large sliver of crisp skin in his mouth.

When the Colonel, smirking, makes a remark about my father's deferment, Grandmother feels a faint coming on and we drop our voices while Grandfather revives her with a glass of sherry from the sideboard. I lean against Aunt Myrtle—Woodhue perfume, tinkle of gold bracelets—and gaze longingly at Uncle Paul, eyes now fully closed against his mysterious pain.

Grace is about to be said. Aunt Ethel, belly tight against the table, sighs that she'll have no one there when the baby comes and reaches for her husband's hand, which moves away. Almost tenderly, my father takes up her other hand and the hand of my mother and winks at me.

She is happy, She is gay.
That is why we
Love her this way—

Aunt Ethel writes this in my autograph book when I'm seven. By then, I've guessed that the Rogersons depend on me to be attentive and high-spirited. I watch the clock to be sure my mother wakes from her long afternoon nap in time for dinner, bring cool cloths to soothe Grandfather's headaches after work, and put on a good dress for the table. I pray that Uncle Paul and Aunt Myrtle will visit with their friends who, like them, dress glamorously and drink cocktails and smoke in front of my grandparents. Why hadn't I been adopted by them? My mother says they drink and dance at a casino every weekend and will ruin themselves.

The Death of My Uncle

My uncle's childhood bedroom has a closed door, whereas my mother's and aunt's have been turned into guest rooms. I go in stealthily to look at his sailboats and construction sets, collections of arrowheads, the little sailor suits pressed and hung in the closet, and report cards arranged in a bookcase. His photograph portrays the handsomest young man I've ever seen.

I learn about his illness by eavesdropping on whispered conversations. He has a bad stomach, then ulcers, a surgery and more surgeries. Something is eating his stomach. He's in and out of the hospital. I send impassioned drawings of suns and rainbows to cheer him. One day, I'm allowed to visit. From a rocking chair, my beautiful uncle smiles crookedly.

Uncle Paul

Mistaking him for an old woman, I shrink away. My mother pushes me forward and my latest drawing slips out of his grasp. I never see him again, but I continue to station myself around corners to hear the reports— he can't get out of bed, then, can't eat, won't talk, won't open his eyes, can't stop hiccupping. I'm shocked to hear doctors have suggested "putting him under" to remove his teeth, "make him more comfortable," I come to think of death as a huge bird devouring its prey.

Childhood Illnesses

My mother, perhaps because she has to wait so many years for an adoption, appears to rely on the childrearing techniques propounded in a book by Dr. Herman N. Bundesen, one I discover in her nightstand and pore over. His very name sounds like the buntings that constrain babies. The infant, he advises, needs to be protected from scratching himself or sucking his fingers by having the long sleeves of the sleeping gown pinned to the crib sheet. The bowel is to be "trained" as early as 2 months but no later than 6 months, by clamping a pot against the child's buttocks at the same time every day. For strength and health, a daily dose of cod liver oil is necessary. "Place the infant on your lap," he instructs, "and open its mouth by gently but firmly pressing its cheeks together between thumb and fingers, holding it open so he can't spit up." (*Our Babies*, 1933)

As early as three and four, I have surgeries on tonsils, adenoids, and appendix, and contract rheumatic fever that doctors say has affected my heart. Subjected to suffocating chloroform masks and to unpleasant poking and potions to make me well again, I spend long days and nights in bed gripped by terror of dying like my uncle.

To protect my heart, doctors restrict walking. I'm carried to the bathroom and to meals by my father, taken out for air in a buggy and teased as a "baby" by neighbor kids. Alone in bed, I escape in an invisible car.

The Country

As I'm turning six, we move to a rural town twenty miles away, living temporarily in the first house built there, vacant for years. Story-book like, it has four-poster canopy beds with trundle beds underneath, bureaus stuffed with hand-stitched clothing and wreaths woven from women's hair. Door lintels have carved crosses to ward off witches, and the basement, we're told, has a sealed tunnel that was part of the underground railway for slaves to escape to Canada. I summon courage once to go down, pushing my brother ahead of me, but our exploring is cut short by sticky cobwebs, dead mice underfoot, an awful stench.

Enjoyment of the house is limited by its draftiness and poor heating. That winter, my brother and I huddle downstairs before the fireplace in makeshift beds. The frailer one, I am sometimes put to bed in the south wing, its air thought to be healthier. Nightmarish hours alone in a high bed, murmurs snaking up through floor boards, evergreen fingers tapping the windows. When my father finally finishes repairs on our house across the street, my brother and I, he ill with pneumonia, are pulled over on a sled.

Two miles outside a village of fewer than a thousand people—factory workers, tradespeople, proprietors, salesmen, teachers, two doctors and a lawyer—our house is considered "in the boonies" and my brother and I are bussed to school. Our father dresses in a white shirt and tie to make his rounds selling insurance and he and my mother socialize only with townspeople. School friends all live in town.

My next twelve years will be spent mainly on tar-patched and dirt roads that run past acres of grape vineyards, crop fields, and trampled pastures. It's the 1940's and children are free to roam.

The Salesman

One of the town's popular people, our father collects payments from housewives during the day; evenings, with husbands home, sells policies. Our mother, depressed and lonely in the country, wants my brother and me close by. I can still see her lined face, heavy body sagging against the door frame, as I run across the street to play. She is also a taskmaster, another reason to flee.

The role of a salesman's wife is not enviable: Mondays, she washes and dips his shirts in blueing and starch. Tuesdays, irons a week's worth, fussing over shirtsleeves. Nine o'clock each morning he stands by the door while she tucks a fresh handkerchief in his pocket, goes over him with a brush, straightens his bowtie, and purses her lips for a kiss. Housewives on his route say he's "stepped out of a bandbox." Evenings when he calls on husbands, he accepts a few drinks to be polite. We're usually asleep when the car makes its way into the driveway and parks askew, sometimes in a flowerbed.

Bad Behaviors

When confined indoors, I read books and magazines—Life, The Saturday Evening Post, National Geographic. I never miss The Watch Bird, a cautionary cartoon that appears in a women's magazine. Each month a particular type of naughtiness is featured, "squirming" for example. The cartoon shows two birds, one glaring at the miscreant, the other "watching YOU":

> *Squirmers never sit still. This one in the picture squirmed so much we couldn't tell whether it was a boy or a girl.*

For a child who takes Sunday School lessons to heart and with a mother who enforces proper behavior, the cartoon contributes to what will become an abiding sense of being watched. I am clumsy and too hasty, at 6 or 7 still a bed-wetter, as well as a squirmer, a sneak, and a liar.

I've imagined God as an Eye in the Sky, judging as well as protecting me. The Watch Bird, however, hangs around the house. Sees me at the table sneaking food into my napkin, catches me sniffing my father's cigarette lighter under his roll-top desk and stealing pens, enlists my brother to tattle on me. While the Eye in the Sky can make me feel guilty, only I need know about it, but the Watch Bird has to be defeated with the very behaviors it denounces.

Solitary Play

Some of my most intense experiences after our move to the country are solitary. Our property has five acres of woods, bounded by a highway, railroad tracks, a swamp, and a neighbor's vineyard. My parents consider them a safe corral for a restless child. I spend hours alone there, often having to sneak in with wet pants. It hasn't yet occurred to me the woods can be a bathroom.

Those earlier days of being bedridden had left me impatient with my confinement. Free now to explore our woods, I'm eager to escape the tedium of family routines and play out the stories I read and make up. Sundays are especially boring—after church, a heavy meal of chicken and biscuits and desserts, then naps, all of us in separate rooms. One spring day, flooded fields across the street ripple and shine and I slip out the back door, still in my pink eyelet Easter dress, pull my father's boots over shiny new Mary Janes, and run across to wade in the shallow lake. When wind whips up waves that soak the hem of my dress, I tuck it up and go deeper, pretending Tom the Chimney Sweep and the Water Babies are swimming beneath me — until mud grabs and swallows a boot and I fall flat.

Diana

In third grade, stories about mythology provide me with an imaginary self: Diana, fearless and genderless protector of wild animals and woodland. I choose her over the other goddesses, drawn to her tomboy looks, the short tunic and high boots. Although depicted carrying a quiver of arrows, she is not hunting, but leaping through woods, a small stag beside her, like the spaniel that always accompanies me. As Diana, I have power and purpose and no longer feel so vulnerable before the Eye in the Sky.

The author as Diana

Diana's home in our woods is a myrtle patch where under a stone tablet, we've been told, a servant and her young daughter are buried. Sensing a bond, I dig up my favorite wild flowers—red and white trillium, violets, and jack in the pulpit and transplant them there.

Country Kids

Our near neighbors are a family of eight children. The step-father of the oldest three, an ill-humored man, works the night shift at the canning factory and rises late to do field work before his next shift. His heavy, erratic step on the stairs scatters children. Mrs. O'Malley oversees the fields and migrant workers from early morning until dark and puts her oldest daughter Sandy in charge of the house and young kids. Joe, four years older than me, takes care of the barn animals and machinery. Jessie, three years older and my idol, is clever at escaping work.

Sandy sweeps, washes, irons, cooks, churns, tends the kitchen garden and screams at the kids to help her or get out of the way. Whenever she's out of the way, we riot in the house, invading the closed-off best parlor with its red velour sofa, spinet piano, and china curios, trailed by cats and dogs and the soggy-diapered baby. We commence a circus of eating pie and cake swiped from the kitchen larder, leaping on furniture, pounding piano keys, and setting the pendulum of the grandfather clock off kilter. When we hear Sandy in the kitchen, we slide the oak pocket-doors quietly closed and take off. Since the front parlor is opened only for ceremonial events such as a graduation or a funeral, Sandy is held responsible for the moldy food scraps, missing silverware, dried up turds, and breakage.

Before our move to the country, I'd thought of myself as frail. I wasn't allowed to exercise and was plagued with scary sensations: dizziness, a jumpy heartbeat, shortness of breath, wobbly legs, upset stomach, and, worst of all, a feeling of being outside my body. The casual physical daring of the O'Malleys is contagious. I join in games of wrestling, racing, leaping and climbing. I learn not to be bluffed by dizziness, to trust my legs to lift me over barbed wire and rebound from jumping off a shed roof. I begin to believe that I'm not destined to be sedentary and die.

My brother and I envy the freedom of the O'Malleys. In our home, we're held to strict routines around meals and chores:

Left alone in the shadowy dining room, the door to the kitchen pulled close, whether to punish me or improve my concentration, only she knows, I go on refusing to clean my plate. Bored with the mashed potato castle, peas stashed in the dungeon, skinned-over gravy moat, I train my eyes beyond the mock orange bush and the row of Scotch pine trees, across the street to where the O'Malley kids are playing "kick the can." Their shouts turn to hoots of laughter as we hear Grampa Hanrahan's rattletrap clanking and backfiring down the hill. The old Ford pulls into their driveway, cuts its engine with explosive farts, and creaks open its door. A shriveled old man climbs out and stoops over the bushels of tomatoes for sale. Straightening up, he shouts, "Com'on ya sissies." Laughter turns into squeals as he scoops up tomatoes and hurls them. At the window, I slide back and forth to see around the mock orange bush and enjoy "the great tomato war."

Suddenly, a scream. When he's outgunned, "Handy" is vicious, throwing stones at our tender parts. We've learned that when he calls "you, girlie," and beckons one of us to bring him a beer or ice cream bar, he's hoping to lure us close enough to deliver a painful and embarrassing pinch.

Just as Mrs. O'Malley is flying down the porch steps to collar him, my mother approaches the dining room door. I hurriedly capture a mess of food in my napkin and shove it into the pocket of my dungarees. Surveying my plate, she motions me up to my bedroom.

Through the leaves of the big maple, I can make out figures streaking through the shadows of the O'Malleys' yard. There's a light on in Joe's bedroom, which probably means he's pretending he's there. I think about Joe a lot, even though he never pays any attention to me. I admire the way he looks when he comes out to the school bus, hair combed, and I like watching him when he's working in the barn wearing only bib overalls.

It's almost full dark and quiet now across the street. The little ones are probably sucking popsicles on the front porch and the grownups inside eating fresh-killed chicken and biscuits washed down with whiskey. I think a lot about the O'Malley kids, why they're them and I'm me. "A wild lot," I hear it said. My mother is polite but cool when she runs into Mrs. O'Malley and she doesn't allow us to take the kids up to our bedrooms.

Compared to them, I'm a coward. They sass and run out slamming the door. I fall into line when my mother frowns. They get whacks on the head and the strap and threaten to run away. Thinking about running away affects the borders of my room, which suddenly lose solidity and right angles as night washes over them. I have a frightening perception that nothing is holding up the floor of my bedroom, or even the house, and I begin to air-trace the outlines of my walls and ceiling tiles, then stare hypnotically at my glow-in-the-dark picture of Wynken, Blynken and Nod. This calms me, as does the nearby painting "The Light of the World" depicting a sweet-looking child with curly hair and what looks like a wide-brimmed hat—the Christ child according to my mother.

The stairs creak and I spring up, preparing my face to look sorry. The door opens slowly. No one. Then the contorted face of my father, a hand choking his neck, appears sideways in the door frame. He defeats the hand, and comes into the room with his little skip and grin, offering a brownie from supper.

The lights in the hall go on and he disappears like an apparition. My mother looks in my door as she passes, leading my brother to his bath. The familiar falls back into place. I go to sleep wondering what Jessie is cooking up and feeling proud to be her lieutenant.

Jessie's Gang

"Touch the electric fence," she commands us. "Swallow frog eggs. Crawl under the bull's belly." And to me, "Round up the captives."

I collect them—Polly, Chuckie, Kerrie, Tommy, Peggy and my brother—and lead them through the woods to an abandoned packing house, where I push them up rotting stairs to the airless attic littered with mildewed magazines, buzzing softly with stupified bees.

She teeters on a stack of crates, torso stained with iodine, buzzard feathers in a bandanna around her head. The captives kneel. I pass around a cup of purplish liquid. Lion's blood for courage, she thunders, tossing me a wink. Eyes of fallen sky, warrior cheek-

bones. Never again a glance compelling as hers.

The cup holds a mixture of grape juice and lemonade, but Jessie also concocts poisons to use on her "enemy," a name I'm never allowed to know, although she enlists me to help with her experiments. One time, we collect pesticides, rat poisons, and household cleaners. She opens shotgun shells to extract gun powder and with rubber gloves and a mask on mixes the ingredients in a glass canning jar. The two of us inject the fizzing liquid into tomatoes, squash, and melons with fountain pens stolen from my father's desk. Buried under straw in an abandoned chicken coop, they will generate heat and ignite the gun powder, she promises. I wake each morning with anticipation but when after a week nothing happens and they begin to rot in ordinary ways, Jessie loses interest.

It's Jessie who imparts information that gets me into trouble when I tell a version of it to my school friends who tell their mothers: this occurs on a hot day, as, sprawled on the bank of the horse pond, we're smearing mud on mosquito bites. She grabs a stick with a projection on it and thrusts it at me, jeering: *this is what men look like down there*, poking it sharply between thumb and forefinger, *this is what they do to you.*

"You're lying!" I protest. *You just wait,"* she hurls back.

There comes a day when, curled on her bed, her legs bloodied from the strap, she dismisses me with cruel words: *get lost, you're such a baby*. Then she disappears and it's rumored she's run away with an older boy from another town. Hollow with grief, I seem to see her everywhere, disappearing down a school corridor, running in the far pasture, looking over her shoulder for me.

But that is the future and before then, **I, Diana, Protector of Animals**, continue to oversee my woods, although with a keen fear of coming across wounded animals. I've obsessed about hurt and dying animals probably from the age of three or four, when on a family drive, a rabbit runs under our tires and my father stops to "help it." For months, I'm told, I ask about the bunny and refuse to sleep in my own bed.

My father can be counted on to put injured animals, wild and domestic, out of their misery. He is also a hunter, a contradiction I struggle with. I'm excited when hunting season opens and ask to be wakened before dawn to help serve him oatmeal, pancakes, eggs, bacon, and toast, and pack his lunch, while my mother perks strong coffee for his thermos. I assist him in buttoning his stiff canvas hunting coat with the red patch on the back, and whistle up the neighbor's beagle waiting outside. I race my brother to be first when they return.

I'm still under the influence of childhood stories the first time I thrust my hand into his game pocket, recoiling from the sensation of cold fur and a stiff body. He lays the rabbit out on the butcher block. I stand as far away as I can and still see while he strips off the skin as one would a baby's snowsuit, peeling it down the legs, pulling it inside out over the tiny feet. I never get over my shock that farm kids take butchering as a matter of course. One time, I'd come upon the O'Malley kids chasing a stuck pig with excited whoops and thereafter approach barnyards with extreme caution.

When my father kills our chickens, I stay inside until my brother comes to tell me "they didn't suffer and they're really dead this time." Then, I join them to help with the plucking and cleaning. Once in an ef-

The author and her brother about to pluck chickens

fort to spare my feelings, my father promises to use a gentler technique. Usually he stands at the edge of a depression in our barnyard, clamps a squawking body between his legs, slits the throat, and tosses the chicken into the pit where it thrashes to death. With his new method, he promises, death will be instantaneous. He ties several by a leg to a tree limb, opens each beak and makes a cut in the throat with a small penknife. Not a squawk or twitch. I watch, between fingers spread over my eyes, awed by the peaceful process. That is, until the rope breaks and, without a cluck, the chickens stagger off into the woods. The scene must have lodged deep in my brain, for years later at a performance of Beethoven's Ninth Symphony when the chorus launches into the Ode

to Joy, those walking dead reappear as a host, wings extended, ascending skyward.

Around the age of eight or nine, I have another experience so traumatic I partially repress it. Tagging after an older cousin on my uncle's beef farm, I follow him into the slaughterhouse where I'm assailed by high-pitched screams and glimpses of staggered and downed cows, brilliant red blood swirling into drains, and men in black rubber aprons looming over them. I don't know if I scream or faint, or try to run, but I remember a voice thundering, "For Chrissake, get her out of here" and that is all I will remember for years except in ghastly nightmares.

Judy Garland
and the Road to Hollywood

I go to her movies with my family and practice her songs, prancing in front of the living room mirror, waving a dust rag. Hollywood is the way to go, I think, and never doubt my talent. My confidante is Mr. Carter in the corner drug store. Saturdays, after chores, I march the mile and a half into town, singing out to passing tractors, "Howdy Farmer, Happy Harvest."

In crisp white shirt and sleeve guards, Mr. C. gives me his usual welcome from behind the soda fountain. "Sit down, Miss Judy, and shake off the dust of the road." Brings to my table a sundae with extra hot fudge, whipped cream, crushed peanuts, and two cherries. His treat. I talk about my fabulous future and how I'll never wear mink coats or ride in limousines and will give pots of money to the poor, including him. "Obliged," he nods. He may be interviewed about me, I inform him. "I'll tell them that when you lived here, we called you Freckles." "Mr. Carter," I shriek, "Well, you could say instead that I was forced to work in hot fields." "I could say that," he considers, resuming his crossed-arm stance behind the counter. When I curl up beside the mag-

azine rack with Silver Screen, he warns, "Be careful not to bend pages, Miss Judy, and mind you straighten the rack when customers come in."

The Grape Post

Sometime around the same age, on one of my trips to the drugstore, along a road lined with grape vineyards, I have what I come to think of as a vision. Striding along bareheaded under midday sun, I feel a shift—both within and without. A tremendous energy radiates from my chest and connects to objects around me—grape leaves and stones are animated. My attention fixes on an arbor post, its rough surface pulsing. As it splits open, I see the face of my Sunday School Jesus with deep wood grain furrows in his cheeks. The sense of being connected to a power not of this world becomes a secret comfort.

The Mission

Caught between painful self-consciousness at school and the claustrophobia of our house, I broaden my exploring, leaving our woods for nearby fields and farms where being alone feels risky. Gun reports, deserted barns, eerie bird shrieks, gruff farmers who wave me off their land — anything can startle me into a clumsy run. Compelled to be outside no matter what the weather, I imagine lives that depend on me, the perceived task of my earlier childhood. I don't remember most of the stories I invent, but I can still visualize the stations of my route. In one secluded spot, I stand on a crate, my version of the UN podium, and denounce Stalin.

The Circuit

I leap off the back porch steps, dash around the corner and over the highway into the pine trees on the edge of a neighbor's wheat field. Hoping not to encounter his crippled son with a hare lip who might limp over to talk to me, I race over paths toward the creek where it stretches out of sight of my house. At a bend, a backless kitchen chair is planted beside the water. Here, I'd imagined a crazy man like one of the people in the county home where our grade school chorus gave a concert. While we were being treated to cookies and punch, I nervously eyed patients in pajamas, pulling at their clothes, grimacing, and twitching. Their agitation seemed to mirror my inner nervousness and I thought: *I could end up here!*

At the edge of the creek bank, I force myself to peer over at the jerry-built structure of scrap wood

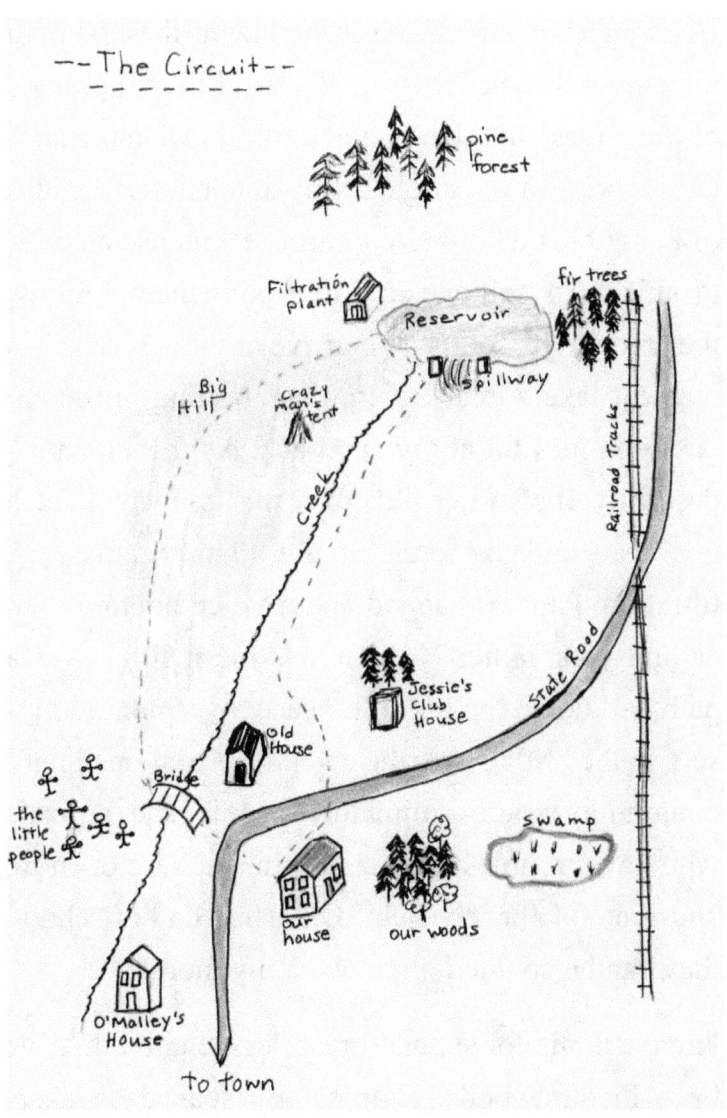

and tarps, then pace by the water to give the man a chance to come out. I hope in time he will trust me. Mostly, I want to learn how he came to be crazy and see the inside of his tent.

Heading on toward the reservoir, the furthest point of my circuit, I look across a field to a hill with a stand of pine trees, tall, dense, and dark. As Diana, guardian of forests, this should be my domain, but the idea of being outside my circuit arouses intense anxiety. Promising myself one day I'll explore them, I follow the creek to its source and arrive at the reservoir—a magical lake. Great Blue herons nesting in the encircling pines lift at my approach. After rain, an iridescent veil of water falls over the spillway. I catch my breath and take in the beauty, all mine, unless the filtration plant is manned and a voice booms, "I'm calling your father," which sets me racing, over a path and down the big hill, nearly overrunning myself, to the bridge over the creek where an imaginary community waits—miniature people and animals who have troubles similar to mine and are open to, and grateful for, my help. On a bad day at school, they can be counted on to boost my morale.

I arrive home for supper, breathless, claiming, "I've been in our woods," hoping my soaked sneakers won't give me away.

Country Girls (and Boys)

School over, we burst into summer, careening down hills on bicycles, no brakes. And we go nearly naked in halters, shorts, no underwear. Skin blistered, then browned, feet sticky black with tar, we're dog-spider-wasp-and snake-bitten, horse-thrown, skunk-sprayed, BB-stung, Indian-burned. Daring each other, we leap off shed roofs and into swimming holes until one summer we begin to dab tropical colors on lips and nails and smudge our lids with purple eye shadow.

More aware of boys and my body, I become excessively self-critical. One day, staring at what I think is a very unattractive dark-shadowed school portrait, I notice how broad my nose is. Like those of African women in National Geographic or a picture of Aunt Jemima. My parents claim they don't remember what my birth mother looked like, but now I decide they know something they don't want me to find out. For a while, especially when I'm reading, I pinch my nose together in an effort to reshape it.

Too soon, the privacy and sanctity of Diana's woods are invaded by town friends who bring their BB guns. Tee shirts off, boys race over a clearing while others aim at their backs. In "outlaw" games, we girls let ourselves be captured. It's not long before BB guns are traded for 22's. Our fathers have trained us in gun safety and trust us to shoot only at targets and pests like crows and squirrels.. This creates a crisis: I can't condone or witness killing. I avoid what I dread, but not always:

I'm in the woods waiting for him to come along, whistling, his twenty-two over his shoulder— my friend's older cousin, blue-black hair, crane legs, a scent like laundry in a March wind. Hoping he'll let me trail him, springing lightly on the balls of my feet as he does. I'm thrilled by his cocksureness, thrilled when he holds back a branch or puts out a warning palm. Eager for the moment when he hands me the gun and, arms around me, helps me sight a target. Praying we won't see animals like the day he shot a vulture picking at a deer carcass and whooped into the field, hoisting the bird on a stick and flinging it up over and over. With covered eyes, I could sense how sun rayed from him and moved like a sleeper to join him.

The Pine Forest

As puberty and my sense of being "different" intensifies my moods, my mother grows concerned. She waylays me as I head out the door and sometimes follows me down the driveway trying to get me to talk. I pull away; I can't tell her how much I'm oppressed by her strict opinions, nor can she, I think, possibly understand my anguish at not being one of the popular girls. Getting away from her is crucial, a matter of even more subterfuge and swiftness. When she's in another room, I leap off the porch, a sharp right, a flat-out run and a dash across the highway, her calls receding in the distance.

Even at the time, I'm not proud of these betrayals of her, she who through all my illnesses has been by my side, reassuring me I won't die, interpreting God as a friendly father. She is the first to instruct us in God's intentions, particularly regarding conduct, and is more to the point than our rambling Methodist minister: No, she says, God does not punish bad behaviors of children. He leaves that to parents. Despite what Pastor Campbell and our Catholic friends say, she does not believe He will put anyone in Hellfire, even our beloved chicken-killer dog. The end of the world will not come in our lifetime and we need not worry about death—ours is years away and will occur in our sleep. About Heaven, she knows little, but trusts we four will always be together.

In later years, she will come to mind purified of ambivalence--on her knees in the garden picking sun-warmed strawberries for our breakfast cereal, up late at night sewing a dress for me, working out our splinters, tending injured birds, helping our dogs whelp. She lies on the bed every night to read to us, holds our foreheads when we're sick, holds our father through his dreadful kidney stone attacks. But by my early adolescence, her "sacrifices" and endless toil, provoke guilty resistance.

One late afternoon in a chilly spring with snow still on the ground, anguish compels me to find a place where nobody can find me, but where I will be understood. For a long time, I've paused at the farthest point of my circuit to look toward the distant stand of pine trees. On this day, tears of self-pity blinding me, I take off across unfamiliar stubble fields.

Sun bursts through the grey sky just as I reach them, and shafts of golden light slant like arrows between their trunks. I fall down on the spongy carpet, stretching out my limbs and lapping at pine-scented snow.

An unearthly sighing from the back of the woods causes me to look up and see the contours of a huge boulder. I feel compelled to approach it, but wind moans and moves in the darkening trees, and fear and chill overcome me. Then I see my mother bending over the refrigerator to pull out vegetables for dinner, worrying about where I am. Feeling pity and relief, I scramble up and race for home vowing I will eat nothing for supper, having received a "Sign." I make a promise to come back. And although I never do, I continue for a number of years to think of the boulder and the pine forest as the fearful passage into death that awaits me.

A Child's Notions

By the age of 10 or so, I've patched together beliefs to help manage my anxiety about death and injury of animals and people. The natural world is a domain in which I have some power. The price I pay is vigilance—having to hold in mind whoever or whatever I know or think to be in distress—a task that involves endless obsessing and sleeplessness. If I imagine winter storms have trapped deer without food, I deprive myself of an extra blanket. Or give up dessert. None of my sacrifices lasts very long. I seem to be satisfied by my intentions.

I have rituals and superstitions to prevent harm: tearing along on my bike with a tractor-trailer coming up behind me, I speed up, thinking, "If I pass the concrete marker before he passes me, my motherfatherbrother will be safe." I recite parts of the catechism learned from Catholic friends. Sleeplessness is a major problem. Afraid to be awake when others are sleeping but afraid to let myself relax into sleep, which feels like falling into a pit, I pester my brother in an adjacent room, until he yells, "Thanks a lot! Now *I* can't go to sleep!" Then it's safe to drop off.

During those young years I don't see a need to reconcile Diana with a Christian God, or wonder how the latter can be an Eye in the Sky. My notions about my biological mother, and therefore myself, are similar patchworks, but cut from conventional cloths. My brother and I are the only adopted children I know about. From story books, I've come to think of adoptees as orphans who are "lucky to have found a good home and need to be grateful." All I know about my birth mother is that she was 19 and not married and in those days in a small town that meant "from the wrong side of the tracks." I enlarge on this, imagining her promiscuous and homeless.

My Mother, Grace

In my growing-up years, I think of her as "above" me. Not only is her family wealthy, but she, chronically depressed, can be distant or disapproving. She is the rock of the extended family, and none of us notices her fault lines and erodings until, in her early sixties, she collapses and dies within two weeks. Cancer, doctors say. I know better. She has worn out.

During childhood I'm alert to her sighs, which range from light exhalations of weariness to sounds of despair when she thinks she's alone— in her bedroom or rock garden, in a back room ironing. They seem addressed to a life that doesn't fit her. When they sound angry, I fear she might leave us, but most dreadful are those hoarse irregular sounds uttered during naps when, features collapsed, she seems beyond the reach of anyone.

She dies two weeks after my husband and I adopt our first child. As she labors to breathe in a hospital bed, a nurse urges me, "Call her, she can hear you." Despite opening my mouth and straining to speak, I remain mute, flashing back to those afternoons as a child when I sat willing her to wake up. Making arrangements for her funeral, I dread viewing her face and ask that her casket be closed. The funeral director demurs, saying that people will be disappointed and furthermore they will think that "something was wrong."

The day after her funeral, I have a dream that makes my unconscious image of my birth mother startlingly clear. As in a fairy tale, I'm walking through wintry woods, cradling my starving infant daughter when I come upon a small hut. A witch-like woman appears—dirty black hair, torn blouse, one breast exposed—and offers to nurse my baby. Repelled, certain of my mother's disapproval, I turn away and trudge on into the storm. Better death than disgrace.

Discovering Dorothy

Although I'd been told about my adoption early on, only as an adult when I meet Dorothy will I understand how physical differences from my mother contributed to a sense of being wrong and out of step. Dorothy, I will discover, does not sit still. She jumps up to tend to something, sits abruptly down again, only to hop up to take care of something else.

Hopelessly out of step with my slow-paced parents, I dread family strolls. In Dorothy, I will find my mirror. But it will be too late to significantly alter my self-consciousness. Through adolescence and beyond, I spend hours fussing futilely with limp hair (like hers). High school friends dub me "Kanga", or "kangaroo" because of my quick awkward gait.

Years after the death of both my parents, I'm standing one day beside their graves when a name pops into my head as if on a movie screen, **Ruckh**, the name I had seen on official papers related to my adoption when, long ago, I'd snooped through my father's files. I remember thinking how strange that name looked with its triple consonants, remember sounding it out--"rook?" A black bird?

The name takes me to my city's public library about fifty miles from the town where I'd grown up. There's an M. Ruckh in its phone book. Not sure if I want to reveal myself, I explain to the trembling voice that answers: "I'm doing a family tree and have reason to think you may know a relative of mine. Do you know a Dorothy Ruckh?"

"Oh my yes," the woman breathes, "she's my sister-in-law!"

She rushes on to tell me that Dorothy married a boy from my home town—and has four children in the area! She runs to look up addresses and telephone numbers. Dorothy and her husband now live in Florida, oddly, close to my in-laws.

In response to a short note with my "family tree" story, Dorothy writes that I can telephone her. A youthful voice answers and calls out, "Grandmother," so I know I will have to be circumspect. Chest tight, heart beating in my ears, I ask questions that I think Dorothy can answer without giving herself away to her family. She tells me that she and her husband lived for a while with his parents. Her mother-in-law, I realize, was my piano teacher. Could we have crossed paths? Our conversation begins to lag and I take a plunge, tell her I was adopted, tell her where and when I'd been born.

"Do you think," I all but whisper, "we're very closely related?" A long pause. "Well, I don't know," she says, her voice uncertain.

I have plans to be in Florida soon visiting my in-laws, I say, and would like to see her. She thinks she can arrange it. "Goodbye, Judy," she says, and I'm thrilled by her soft voice saying my name.

After our first conversation, Dorothy manages to call without her husband around and tells me that after high school, she along with girlfriends took jobs cleaning summer houses on Lake Erie: "That's when it happened… He was some guy from Cleveland… I didn't tell my parents… I got a room with a lady who was nice to me…the adoption was arranged in the hospital…l don't remember much of all that."

Did she tell her husband? "He learned about it from one of my sisters before we married. He asked if it was true and then said, 'We will never speak of this again.' And we never did."

Wanting to know if we are temperamentally alike, I ask if she is nervous, a worrier. "Oh, yes," she says, "I'm always jumping around. Can't stay in one spot. And I worry all the time—about the children and grandchildren."

After we hang up, I imagine years of getting to know Dorothy. In the months before I'm to meet her, I'm giddy with anticipation, like someone chosen to appear on the TV show, "This is Your Life" with a mystery guest sweeping in from the wings.

The Meeting

A doll-like woman stands on the steps of a diner, turning in all directions. That can't be Dorothy. She's too short and doesn't look at all like me. But it is. I guide her inside, already feeling more like her mother than her daughter. Across from her in a booth, looking deeply into her face and uncertain which questions to ask first, I have an odd sensation: "I'm looking at my own nose," I say with surprise. "Oh yes," she says, "We have a Belgian nose. Short and wide."

And even though I can't see that I really look like her, I'm struck by her gestures, tapping foot, quick fluttery movements. How reassuring it is to see someone who moves like me. All my life I've blamed myself for being high-strung, when all along I've simply been the child of this quick, birdlike woman.

Our brief hour together is as exciting as any real or imagined tryst. She tells me she has thought of me every day of her life. Tears shine on her cheeks. My hands reach to pick up and cradle her small fingers. We talk excitedly, exchanging light touches.

We may not see each other again and I want details about her life. She obliges by telling me she loves to dance (they go to the Legion), likes baseball, and likes "to take a drink." "Do you?" she asks, "like to take a drink?" (Later I will learn from her daughters that she hides cigarettes and beer from her husband.)

Her slight body animated, nearly levitating, she talks on, tells me she is legally blind from macular degeneration and can no longer even cook—and she drove to see me!

That hour with Dorothy in the diner is like coming upon a treasure intended for me alone. She feels like a child of my heart, her story so poignant that I can

Dorothy and the author

imagine being there at my own birth, gripping her hand, reassuring her she's doing the right thing and that I will find her later on.

Although I hold back from asking, I am of course very eager to know who my father is, but in this

I am, and will remain, disappointed, for Dorothy says vaguely, she can't remember. Some Italian boy, she adds. I know not to push her. It seems she was also confused about whom she'd given birth to: "a red-haired boy," she says she told her husband. Too soon, she announces she has to return to him with an excuse for her unusual time away. While I pay the bill, she flits around the candy display, selects a chocolate mint, and smooths the wrapper to take home-- "as a souvenir," she smiles shyly.

In the parking lot, I pull out my camera and a stranger strolls over offering to take our picture. Dorothy leans into me, her head barely above my shoulder. As she starts toward her car, I call out to her impulsively, wanting to delay her, "I have another question: Does your nose always run, like mine?" "Oh my yes," she says, "I carry tissues all the time."

"Happy Birth-day, Judy," I say as I drive away.

That night in my motel room I fall into a dream in which I'm standing alone on the edge of a dance floor. A tall black man comes forward and, with a silent nod of invitation, leads me into the middle of the floor. I remember thinking it remarkable that not only can I dance, I who always have had two "left hoofs," but that as I press into him, my body expands to fit his— two halves of a perfect whole.

Afterwards, I write her: "I was happy to see many of my features and gestures reflected in you. It was deeply satisfying to meet you and I have an inner calm I did not have before."

On my next visit to Florida, Dorothy introduces me to her husband and he and I reminisce about our home town. We make plans to celebrate Dorothy's eightieth birthday the following year. I write her: "I am grateful for the warmth and ease I feel with both of you. I hope, Dorothy, that you will have no further anxiety about me or because of me. I owe you my life, you know, and it is a good one."

"Sad news," her husband tells me when I arrive the next year. "Dorothy's in the hospital with brain cancer. She would like to see you."

He sits slumped in a chair beside the bed where she lies as if embalmed, eyes closed, thin hair lacquered down. "Call to her," he says, "she's been expecting you." And this time, I do call. Dorothy opens her eyes and smiles, says my name. Very gently, I hold her hand, its fingernails polished bright red by her daughters.

Within a month, she's in a nursing home, dying. Her four children gather around her on Mother's Day and their father arrives with five dozen roses and a note: From all your children. When they look confused, he tells them Dorothy's secret. Her daughters weep that she felt she had to conceal it.

I attend the burial of Dorothy's ashes in her home town. At the service her two daughters entwine their arms in mine as we all sing *Amazing Grace*.

r. to l.: the author with her half-sisters, Dale Ann and Dawn

Birth Mother

The wind is harsh in this cemetery.
Only a small group has gathered
for the burial of her ashes.

Sixty years ago, she handed me over
without remembering my sex
or the color of my hair.
A red-haired boy, she told the man she wed.

But I looked and found her in later years
and was pleased to notice
her nose and brow were like mine,
as was her quickness to cry.

When she lay in a nursing home, her brain
unraveling, I'm told she grasped the arm
of a stranger and pulled him to her,
whispering, "I've been a good girl."

I think of an April day when she, nineteen,
living alone in a boarding house,
knew it was time and walked
the several blocks to the hospital.

Each of us places a rose on the grave.
Now when it's too late, I long to offer her
a child's fistful of dandelions,
sleep in the curve of her body.

Afterword

Decades later, the current of my days quickening, I pull on a sweater and take a path along a creek to my office. Arms swinging, feet picking up the pace, I could be the child on her way to town, dreaming of recognition.

Today is the first day of school, young children stand waiting for their bus and a collective throb of excitement and anxiety is palpable. In the "autobiography" I wrote when 12, I would be a war correspondent, following in the footsteps of Marguerite Higgins or, study agriculture and animal husbandry, making great breakthroughs for my farming friends. My high school vocational tests will point to missionary work abroad.

A Great Blue heron stands still in the shallows of the creek and I'm reminded of my old reservoir with the heron rookery and long summer days when I wandered in a trance of expectations. I pause to watch the children, some eager, some hanging back, as they move toward the open door of the bus, each embarking on a singular journey.

Acknowledgements

I wish to acknowledge the expert and generous help of my publisher Len Kagelmacher; my poetry group of over 30 years; and Carl Dennis, a valued mentor.

Earlier versions of "My Beginnings" as well as "Country Girls," and "Birth Mother" appeared in *The Wind Turning Pages*.

—Judith Slater

www.ingramcontent.com/pod-product-compliance
Lightning Source LLC
Chambersburg PA
CBHW070440010526
44118CB00014B/2129